ARTICLES TO GUIDE FRIENDSHIPS INTO MORE

ALYSSA HATHAWAY

ARTICLES TO GUIDE FRIENDSHIPS INTO MORE

Advise the Heart

organizations are unintentional.

Not Legal or Financial Advice: This book is not intended to serve as a source of legal, business, accounting, or financial advice. Readers are strongly encouraged to seek the guidance of qualified professionals in the legal, business, accounting, and financial fields for specific advice and assistance.

Unauthorized duplication or distribution of this material in any form is strictly prohibited. Violators will be prosecuted to the fullest extent of the law.

The author, publisher, and distributor of this product assume no responsibility for the use or misuse of this product, or for any physical or mental injury, damage, and/or financial loss sustained to persons or property as a result of using this report. The liability, negligence, use, misuse, or abuse of the operation of any methods, strategies, instructions, or ideas contained in the material herein is the sole responsibility of the reader.

The material contained in this publication is provided for information purposes only.

NOTICE: We believe that an active and healthy sex life, based on mutual consent and respect between partners, is an important part of a healthy relationship. We also believe in the practice of safe sex, through the use of contraceptives, regular medical examination, or both. Moreover, we respect that sex is a private matter and that each person has a different opinion of what sexual practices, dating etiquette, or beliefs are appropriate. We are committed to offering responsible, professional, and helpful advice about dating and sexual matters. However, this book is intended as a reference only. It is not intended as a substitute for professional advice. Please consult a competent professional for your specific sexual, mental, emotional, medical, or other concerns.

CAUTION: This publication may contain explicit adult content not suitable for anyone who is under the legal age limit.

CONTENTS

CONTENTS

CONTENTS

CONTENTS

SECTION 1 -
FRIENDSHIP
FUNDAMENTALS

THE BASICS ON FRIENDSHIPS

"Nobody's an Island," as the famous line from John Donne's Meditation XVII suggests, we're all interconnected. We can't go it alone on this planet, which is why different kinds of relationships, like friendship, are so important.

Understanding what friendship truly means involves looking at its definitions and why it's so valuable. Take Aristotle, for example. He's a big deal in philosophy and has a lot to say about why friendship matters.

Aristotle's take? No one would choose to live without friends. He argues that even if you have everything else—money, power, status—friends are still the most crucial. After all, what's the point of having all those things if you can't share them with people you care about? Friends aren't just there for the good times; they're your lifeline in tough times too.

Aristotle goes so far as to say that friendship is as vital as life itself. It doesn't matter if you're young or old, rich or poor—friendship is universal. In fact, wealthy folks might need friends even more, because what's wealth without someone to enjoy it with? Plus, having friends can reduce life's risks; when unexpected things happen, your friends are there to help.

But here's the real kicker: friendship inspires you to be a better person. Being around friends encourages positive thoughts and actions. Even when helping out isn't easy, there's a sense of joy in it because you're doing it for someone you care about. And in that process, you grow as a person too.

So, having friends isn't just about fun and games; it's about becoming the best version of yourself and building meaningful connections that last a lifetime.

Imagine waking up knowing you have friends who've got your back no matter what. It's like having a support system built right into your life, ready to celebrate your victories and lift you up during challenges.

Aristotle believed that true friendship isn't just about hanging out or sharing stuff; it's about uplifting each other. When you're with friends, you naturally want to do good things. It's like they bring out the best in you, inspiring you to be kinder, more generous, and just overall a better person.

And it's not just about the big moments; it's the little things too. Like having someone to laugh with over silly jokes, or being able to talk about your dreams and fears without judgment. These everyday moments build the foundation of a strong friendship.

One of the beautiful things about friendship is that it's a two-way street. You give, and you receive. Whether it's a shoulder to lean on or a cheerleader in your corner, friends add richness and depth to your life that money can't buy.

And let's not forget the fun part! From spontaneous adventures to cozy nights in, the memories you create with friends are priceless. It's these shared experiences that make life truly meaningful.

So, if you're ever wondering why friendship matters, just remember this: it's not just about having someone to hang out with. It's about having someone who makes life brighter, challenges you to grow, and reminds you that you're never alone on this journey.

IDENTIFY WHERE YOUR FRIENDSHIPS HAVE ISSUES

Making and keeping good friends is such a rewarding part of life, but let's face it, friendships aren't always smooth sailing. There are bound to be ups and downs along the way, and it's important to navigate through them with care.

When issues arise in friendships, it can feel

tough and unexpected. However, facing these challenges head-on can strengthen your bond in the long run. Understanding where the issues stem from is key to finding solutions and moving forward together.

Communication is the cornerstone of resolving friendship issues. But sometimes, finding the right words or knowing how to proceed can be tricky. Each friendship is unique, shaped by its own circumstances, history, and personalities.

One common issue is when busy schedules get in the way. If you or your friend are caught up in work or other commitments, it can strain your connection. Expressing how you feel about this to your friend can be a step towards resolving the issue and reaffirming your bond.

Another challenge is when friends drift apart due to changes in their lives. It can be disheartening to feel like you've lost the closeness you once had. Talking openly with your friend about these changes can help bridge the gap and keep your friendship alive.

Feeling abandoned without explanation is another tough situation. Seeking closure and understanding why things changed can be important for moving forward, even if it's not always easy to get answers.

Ultimately, addressing friendship issues promptly and honestly can prevent them from escalating. Value your friendships by being aware of potential issues and working together to overcome them, ensuring that your bonds remain strong and meaningful.

Friendship issues often arise unexpectedly, and they can be challenging to navigate. It's like sailing through rough waters—you need to steer carefully to keep your friendship ship afloat.

One common issue is when life gets hectic, and you or your friend struggle to find time for each other. This can lead to feelings of neglect or uncertainty about the strength of your bond. Expressing these feelings honestly can open up a dialogue and pave the way for reconnecting on a deeper level.

Another challenge is when misunderstandings or miscommunications occur. It's easy for words or actions to be misinterpreted, causing rifts in friendships. Taking the time to clarify intentions and listen to each other's perspectives can go a long way in resolving conflicts.

Sometimes, friendships evolve or change naturally over time. This can be bittersweet, especially if you feel like you're growing apart from a close friend. However, acknowledging these shifts and finding new ways to connect can lead to a more resilient and adaptable friendship.

Trust is another vital aspect of friendship, and issues like feeling betrayed or let down can strain even the strongest bonds. Addressing trust issues requires honesty, vulnerability, and a willingness to work through challenges together.

Ultimately, every friendship is unique, and there's no one-size-fits-all approach to resolving issues. What's important is staying open, communicating openly, and being willing to listen and understand each other's perspectives. By doing so, you can navigate through friendship challenges with grace and strengthen your bond along the way.

HOW YOUR FRIENDSHIPS AFFECT YOUR LIFE

One significant way friends can influence us is through our beliefs and values. When we're surrounded by friends who constantly reinforce certain beliefs, whether positive or negative, it can shape how we see the world. For example, if your friends often express pessimism about job opportunities, you might start adopting a negative outlook on the job market without even realizing it.

Our friends can also impact our self-confidence. If our friends hold negative perceptions about us or others, it can affect how we view ourselves. For instance, if your friends label someone as snobbish, you might start doubting your own worthiness based on their beliefs.

Behavior is another area where friends wield influence. Observing how our friends behave can subconsciously influence our own actions. For instance, if you see a friend being polite to others, you might start emulating that behavior without consciously thinking about it.

Moreover, our friends can influence how we react to situations. If we witness our friends experiencing fear or discomfort, it can change our own perceptions and behaviors. For instance, if a friend is afraid of snakes and shares their experience, you might start feeling wary of snakes too, even if you weren't initially afraid.

Emotionally, friends can have a significant

impact. Being around friends who are joyful can lift our spirits, while experiencing their sadness can also affect our mood. However, it's important to remember that we have agency in how we respond to these emotional influences. Offering support and positive advice to friends in need can not only uplift their mood but also contribute to a more positive emotional environment overall.

In essence, friends can profoundly affect how we feel, think, and perceive the world. Being aware of this influence empowers us to choose friendships that align with our values and contribute positively to our well-being.

One of the fascinating aspects of friendship is how it can shape our goals and aspirations. When we see our friends pursuing their dreams or achieving success, it can inspire us to set higher goals for ourselves. On the flip side, if our friends are complacent or stuck in negative patterns, it can hold us back from reaching our full potential.

Friendships also play a crucial role in our decision-making processes. We often seek advice or opinions from friends when faced with important choices. Their input can influence our decisions, sometimes guiding us towards opportunities we might not have considered otherwise.

Moreover, friends can be our sounding boards and sources of feedback. They offer different perspectives and insights, helping us see situations from various angles. This diversity of viewpoints can enrich our understanding and lead to better-informed decisions.

Another significant impact of friendship is on our well-being and mental health. Positive friendships characterized by trust, support, and mutual respect can contribute to our overall happiness and resilience. Conversely, toxic or unhealthy friendships can lead to stress, anxiety, and emotional turmoil.

Friendships also shape our social skills and communication styles. Interacting with friends teaches us empathy, conflict resolution, and effective communication strategies. These skills are invaluable not just in our friendships but also in our professional and personal lives.

Additionally, friends can introduce us to new experiences, hobbies, and perspectives. They broaden our horizons and enrich our lives by exposing us to different cultures, ideas, and ways of thinking.

Ultimately, friendships are a cornerstone of our social and emotional well-being. They influence our choices, attitudes, and behaviors in profound ways. Cultivating positive and supportive friendships can have a transformative impact on our lives, helping us grow, thrive, and navigate life's challenges with resilience and joy.

WHAT MAKES A GOOD FRIEND?

You're absolutely right that there are different types of friends, and no one wants to be with bad friends. Building and maintaining good friendships requires effort and a genuine desire to be there for each other. Let's explore what makes a friend a good friend and how to embody those qualities.

Firstly, a good friend rejoices in your joys

and supports you through your pains. They're not just sympathetic; they're empathetic, sharing in your feelings and experiences. Good friends don't cut ties over disagreements but instead communicate openly and respectfully, understanding that differences of opinion are natural and can strengthen friendships.

Communication is key in maintaining good friendships. Regular contact and checking in with each other show that you value the relationship. Trust is another crucial aspect—a good friend can be trusted implicitly, and they earn your trust in return. This mutual trust creates a sense of security and eliminates fears of betrayal.

In tough times, a good friend stands by your side, offering support and understanding. They don't escalate conflicts but work towards positive resolutions. They defend and protect you, showing that they care deeply about your well-being.

Ultimately, being a good friend means embodying qualities like empathy, trustworthiness, and loyalty. It's about being there for each other through thick and thin, fostering a relationship built on mutual respect and understanding. By practicing these qualities, you not only become a good friend but also contribute to a healthy and fulfilling friendship.

One of the key qualities of a good friend is loyalty. Loyalty goes beyond just being there for the good times; it means standing by your friend's side through challenges and difficulties. A loyal friend is someone you can count on no matter what, and they prioritize your well-being and happiness.

Trustworthiness is another essential trait. Good friends are honest and reliable, and they keep their promises. When you trust a friend, you feel safe sharing your thoughts, feelings, and secrets with them, knowing that they will respect your trust and confidentiality.

Empathy is a hallmark of good friendships. Empathetic friends not only listen to your concerns but also try to understand things from your perspective. They offer support and encouragement, validating your emotions and experiences.

Communication skills are crucial for maintaining healthy friendships. Good friends are open and transparent in their communication, expressing their thoughts and feelings honestly and respectfully. They also actively listen to their friends, showing genuine interest and understanding.

Respect is fundamental in any friendship. Good friends respect each other's boundaries, opinions, and differences. They avoid judgment and criticism, instead choosing to celebrate each other's strengths and uniqueness.

Positivity and encouragement are also vital aspects of being a good friend. Positive friends uplift each other, offer words of encouragement, and celebrate each other's achievements. They provide a source of motivation and inspiration, helping each other grow and thrive.

Lastly, flexibility and adaptability are important in navigating the ups and downs of friendships. Good friends are willing to compromise, forgive, and work through challenges together. They understand that no friendship is perfect, but with effort and understanding, they can overcome obstacles and strengthen their bond.

In essence, being a good friend involves embodying qualities like loyalty, trustworthiness, empathy, effective communication, respect, positivity, and adaptability. These qualities foster healthy, supportive, and fulfilling friendships that enrich our lives and bring joy and meaning to our relationships.

WHAT MAKES A BAD FRIEND?

You're absolutely right that recognizing the difference between a good and bad friend can be challenging but crucial for maintaining healthy relationships. Let's explore some red flags that might indicate a friendship is not good.

One clear sign of a bad friend is opportunism. These individuals are only interested in what they can gain from you, whether it's material possessions, connections, or status. They may disrespect your belongings or boundaries and become defensive when confronted about their behavior.

Another trait of a bad friend is self-centeredness. These friends make everything about themselves, showing little interest in your life, feelings, or experiences. They may constantly brag or seek attention, making it hard to trust or connect with them on a deeper level.

Furthermore, friends who constantly seek pity or sympathy without reciprocating support can be draining and unreliable. They may turn to you for emotional support but fail to offer the same in return when you need it, leaving you feeling neglected or unvalued.

It's essential to be aware of these warning signs and trust your instincts when assessing friendships. Building healthy relationships requires mutual respect, empathy, and support. If a friendship consistently leaves you feeling undervalued, used, or emotionally drained, it may be time to reevaluate and consider distancing yourself from toxic dynamics.

Ultimately, surrounding yourself with genuine, supportive, and trustworthy friends contributes to a happier and more fulfilling social life. It's okay to set boundaries and prioritize relationships that bring positivity and mutual respect into your life.

One significant aspect of bad friendships is inconsistency. These friends may be unreliable, cancel plans frequently, or only reach out when they need something from you. They may not invest time or effort into nurturing the friendship, leaving you feeling unimportant or neglected.

Furthermore, gossip and betrayal are toxic elements in friendships. Bad friends may spread rumors, talk behind your back, or betray your trust by sharing personal information without your consent. These behaviors erode trust and create a negative atmosphere within the friendship.

Moreover, jealousy and competitiveness can poison friendships. Bad friends may feel threatened by your success or achievements, leading to envy or undermining your accomplishments. They may try to outshine you or downplay your achievements, creating a sense of rivalry rather than support.

Additionally, manipulative behavior is a red flag in friendships. Bad friends may use guilt, coercion, or emotional manipulation to get what they want from you. They may pressure you into making decisions or taking actions that benefit them at your expense, disregarding your feelings or well-being.

It's crucial to recognize these warning signs and prioritize your mental and emotional well-being in friendships. Healthy relationships are built on mutual respect, trust, communication, and support. Surrounding yourself with friends who uplift, encourage, and respect you contributes to a positive and fulfilling social circle.

When assessing friendships, consider how you feel when you're with that person. Do they make you feel valued, understood, and supported? Do they respect your boundaries and treat you with kindness and honesty? These are essential questions to ask to cultivate healthy and meaningful connections in your life.

Ultimately, choosing quality over quantity in friendships leads to more fulfilling and enriching relationships. It's okay to let go of toxic or unhealthy friendships and prioritize those that bring positivity, joy, and support into your life.

LEARN TO UNDERSTAND PEOPLE BETTER

Building and maintaining friendships indeed come with responsibilities and efforts. Understanding your friends on a deeper level is key to fostering strong and lasting bonds. Here are some practical steps to enhance your understanding of your friends:

Firstly, taking the initiative to know your

friend's family and other close friends can provide valuable insights into their life and relationships. Spending time with their loved ones can help you understand their upbringing, values, and the dynamics that shape their personality.

Additionally, showing genuine interest in your friend's passions and hobbies can strengthen your connection. Engage in discussions about their interests, listen attentively, and ask thoughtful questions. This not only shows that you care but also allows you to learn more about what brings them joy and fulfillment.

Respecting boundaries is crucial in understanding your friends. While it's important to delve into meaningful conversations, avoid prying into sensitive or personal matters unless they willingly share. Creating a comfortable and safe space for open communication encourages trust and mutual understanding.

Furthermore, observing their likes and dislikes can provide valuable insights into their preferences and values. Pay attention to their reactions, gestures, and choices in different situations. This awareness helps you navigate interactions and support them in meaningful ways.

Ultimately, understanding your friends involves active listening, empathy, and respect for their individuality. By taking the time to know them on a deeper level, you strengthen the foundation of your friendship and create meaningful connections that withstand challenges and time.

One powerful aspect of understanding your friends is being aware of their emotions and struggles. Paying attention to their mood changes, body language, and verbal cues can help you empathize with what they're going through. Offering a listening ear without judgment and providing emotional support during tough times strengthens your friendship and shows that you genuinely care about their well-being.

Moreover, understanding your friends' goals, aspirations, and fears can give you valuable insights into their motivations and values. Engage in meaningful conversations about their dreams and ambitions, and offer encouragement and support as they pursue their endeavors. Celebrate their successes and be there to uplift them during setbacks, showing that you're invested in their journey and growth.

Another aspect of understanding your friends is recognizing their strengths and areas for growth. Acknowledge and appreciate their unique talents, skills, and qualities that make them special. Encourage them to embrace their strengths and work together on areas where they want to improve, fostering a supportive and empowering dynamic in your friendship.

Furthermore, understanding your friends' communication styles and preferences enhances effective and harmonious interactions. Some friends may prefer direct and straightforward communication, while others may appreciate more subtle cues or gestures of affection. Adapt your communication approach to resonate with their style, promoting clear and meaningful exchanges that nurture mutual understanding.

Additionally, understanding your friends' boundaries and respecting their space is crucial for maintaining healthy and balanced relationships. Be mindful of their comfort levels in various situations, and always seek their consent before discussing sensitive topics or sharing personal information. Respecting boundaries demonstrates trust, respect, and consideration in your friendship.

In essence, understanding your friends encompasses empathy, active listening, mutual respect, and genuine care. By fostering a deep understanding of each other's thoughts, feelings, and perspectives, you cultivate authentic connections built on trust, support, and mutual growth. These qualities form the foundation of strong and enduring friendships that enrich your life and bring joy and fulfillment to both parties.

THE BENEFITS OF FRIENDSHIPS

Indeed, the value of friendship cannot be overstated. Good friends not only bring joy and companionship but also offer numerous benefits for our emotional and physical well-being.

Spending quality time with good friends can have profound effects on our mental health. It boosts our self-esteem, uplifts our mood, and reduces stress levels. Good friends provide a sense of purpose and belonging, enhancing our overall happiness and well-being. They also offer crucial support during challenging times, helping us cope with traumas and life's difficulties.

Moreover, the positive impact of friendship extends to our physical health as well. Social interactions with friends can lower harmful stress levels, benefiting our heart health, insulin regulation, immune system, and gut function. Having a strong social support network can also boost our immune system and aid in recovery from injuries or illnesses.

However, cultivating and maintaining friendships requires effort, especially in adulthood when responsibilities tend to take precedence. It can be challenging to find friends with similar values and interests amidst busy schedules and commitments. That's why it's essential to prioritize genuine connections and make regular efforts to stay connected with good friends.

Nurturing friendships not only enriches our

lives but also contributes to a healthier and happier existence. Investing time and energy in meaningful relationships is a worthwhile endeavor that reaps invaluable rewards for our overall well-being.

One of the remarkable aspects of friendship is its ability to provide a sense of belonging and acceptance. Good friends create a safe space where we can be ourselves without fear of judgment. This acceptance fosters authenticity and allows us to explore our interests, passions, and vulnerabilities freely.

Friendship also plays a crucial role in our mental resilience. During challenging times, such as periods of loneliness, stress, or uncertainty, friends offer a source of strength and support. They listen without judgment, offer perspective, and provide encouragement, helping us navigate life's ups and downs with greater resilience and optimism.

Moreover, friendships contribute significantly to our personal growth and development. Through interactions with friends, we gain valuable insights, learn from different perspectives, and broaden our horizons. Friends challenge us to step out of our comfort zones, pursue new experiences, and discover hidden talents and strengths.

Beyond individual benefits, strong friendships also enrich our communities and society as a whole. Friendships bridge differences, promote empathy and understanding, and foster a sense of unity and cooperation. In a world often marked by division and conflict, the bonds of friendship remind us of our shared humanity and the power of connection to build a more compassionate and inclusive world.

In essence, friendships are not just pleasant companionships; they are lifelines that nourish our souls, uplift our spirits, and contribute to our overall happiness and well-being. Investing in meaningful friendships is a profound act of self-care and a testament to the enduring power of human connection.

STAYING MOTIVATED FOR MAINTAINING FRIENDSHIPS

Maintaining friendships requires effort and dedication, but staying motivated to nurture these relationships can be a deeply rewarding endeavor. Here are some strategies to help you stay motivated and committed to your friendships:

1.   Reflect on precious memories: Recall the meaningful moments you've shared with your friends, both during happy times and challenging periods. Cherishing these memories can remind you of the bond you share and motivate you to continue nurturing your friendship.

2.   Value their importance: Consider the impact your friends have on your life and imagine how you would feel if they were no longer a part of it. Recognizing their significance can inspire you to prioritize your friendships and invest time and effort in maintaining them.

3.   Understand the effort required: Like any relationship, friendships require time, communication, and effort to thrive. Acknowledge the importance of actively engaging with your friends, supporting them, and being present in their lives.

4.   Show appreciation: Express gratitude for your friends' presence and actions. Say "thank you" when they offer support

or kindness, and reciprocate their gestures of friendship. Small acts of appreciation, such as a heartfelt message or a thoughtful gesture, can strengthen your bond and show that you value their friendship.

5. Stay connected: Make an effort to stay connected with your friends regularly, even if it's through simple gestures like texts, calls, or occasional meet-ups. Consistent communication helps maintain the connection and keeps the friendship strong.

6. Be there in times of need: Show your friends that you're there for them during difficult times. Offer a listening ear, provide support, and be a source of comfort when they need it most. Being a reliable and supportive friend fosters trust and strengthens your bond.

By staying motivated and actively engaging in these strategies, you can nurture your friendships and enjoy the rich rewards of meaningful connections with those who bring joy and support to your life.

When it comes to maintaining friendships, ongoing effort and sincere gestures play crucial roles. Here are additional tips to help you stay motivated and strengthen your friendships:

1. Celebrate milestones: Acknowledge and celebrate important milestones in your friends' lives, such as birthdays, anniversaries, achievements, or significant events. Sending a thoughtful card, organizing a small gathering, or simply offering heartfelt congratulations can show your friends that you care about their happiness and successes.

2. Be understanding and forgiving: Understand that friendships may encounter challenges or misunderstandings along the way. Practice patience, empathy, and forgiveness when disagreements arise. Communicate openly, listen to each

other's perspectives, and work together to resolve conflicts peacefully.

3. Share experiences: Create new memories together by engaging in shared activities or experiences that you both enjoy. Whether it's trying out a new hobby, exploring a new place, or attending events together, these shared experiences strengthen your bond and create lasting connections.

4. Respect boundaries: Respect your friends' boundaries and preferences. Understand that everyone has different needs, schedules, and priorities. Be considerate of their time, space, and personal choices, and avoid imposing expectations or pressure on them.

5. Stay connected virtually: In today's digital age, staying connected with friends has become easier through social media, messaging apps, and video calls. Utilize these platforms to stay in touch, share updates, and maintain regular communication, especially if distance

or busy schedules prevent frequent in-person meetings.

6.   Be a supportive listener: Be a supportive and attentive listener when your friends need to talk or share their thoughts and feelings. Practice active listening, offer empathy and validation, and refrain from judgment or criticism. Letting your friends know that you're there to listen and support them can strengthen trust and deepen your bond.

7.   Express kindness and generosity: Show kindness and generosity in your actions and words towards your friends. Offer help when they need it, provide encouragement during challenging times, and extend gestures of kindness, such as small gifts, acts of service, or words of affirmation, to show that you appreciate and value them.

By incorporating these practices into your friendship maintenance routine, you can foster meaningful and enduring connections with your friends, creating a supportive network of mutual care and understanding.

STAYING ON TRACK

Maintaining friendship is indeed a continuous effort that requires genuine interest, active listening, and supportive actions. Here are further insights into staying on track with your friendships:

1.   Be genuinely interested: Show sincere interest in your friend's life, activities, and experiences. Ask meaningful ques-

tions, actively listen to their responses, and engage in conversations that reflect your genuine curiosity and care. Demonstrating your interest helps strengthen the bond and shows that you value their presence in your life.

2.   Support their passions: Encourage and support your friend's passions, hobbies, and interests. Attend their events, cheer them on during their achievements, and participate in activities that they enjoy. Your support not only boosts their confidence but also strengthens your connection as you share meaningful experiences together.

3.   Schedule regular hangouts: Make an effort to schedule regular meetups or hangouts with your friend. Whether it's a weekly coffee date, a monthly movie night, or spontaneous outings, spending quality time together helps nurture your friendship and creates lasting memories.

4.   Communicate effectively: Practice open and honest communication with

your friend. Share your thoughts, feelings, and experiences, and encourage them to do the same. Be transparent about your expectations, boundaries, and concerns, and address any issues or misunderstandings promptly and respectfully.

5.   Stay connected despite distance: If your friend moves to a different location or you both have busy schedules, make an effort to stay connected. Use technology such as video calls, messaging apps, or social media to keep in touch, share updates, and maintain a sense of closeness despite physical distance.

6.   Show appreciation: Express gratitude and appreciation for your friend's presence in your life. Let them know how much you value their friendship, acknowledge their contributions, and express gratitude for the support, laughter, and shared moments you cherish together.

7.   Be reliable and dependable: Be a

reliable and dependable friend by honoring commitments, being there when needed, and offering your support during challenging times. Show consistency in your actions, be trustworthy, and demonstrate that you can be counted on as a true friend.

By staying on track with these practices, you can nurture and strengthen your friendships, creating meaningful connections that last a lifetime.

MAKING RESOLUTIONS FOR FRIENDSHIPS

The upcoming New Year might bring a fresh wave of motivation for changing things up, especially when it comes to your friendships. After all, aren't your friends a big part of what makes life exciting? If not, it's a good time to reflect on the kind of friends you have. Maybe it's about finding the right balance between what they bring to your life and what you bring to theirs. Either way, setting some positive resolutions for your friendships in the New Year could be a great step forward.

Consider letting go of toxic friendships if you want to keep your relationships healthy. You know, those "frenemies" or emotional vampires who always seem to bring you down. Spending too much time with them can mess with your idea of what a good friend really is. Whether you decide to confront them, distance yourself, or simply move on, starting the New Year with a fresh outlook and positive people around you could be refreshing.

Make an effort to spend quality time with your friends. Busy schedules can sometimes get in the way, making it hard to catch up with friends as often as you'd like. It might be time to reassess your priorities, and the beginning of the New Year is a perfect time to do that. Plan regular hangouts or catch-ups with your friends, even if it's just grabbing a coffee or browsing through a store together. The key is to connect personally and enjoy each other's company.

Include thoughts and prayers for your friends in your New Year's resolutions. Even if you can't be together physically, sending positive vibes their way can make a difference. It helps you step back from your own worries and understand your friend's feelings better. This small gesture shows how much you care, even when you're not together. So, wish the best for your friends and watch how it shapes your mindset and strengthens your bonds.

To make the most of your friendships, start by setting positive and nurturing resolutions for the coming year. You've got some great ideas already, so why not add them to your list and see how they brighten up your friendships?

SECTION 2 - MAINTAINING FRIENDSHIPS LONG-TERM

There's a certain allure to being a lone wolf. You have the freedom to indulge in activities you love, whether it's strolling through nature, diving into books, writing poetry, or pursuing solo passions. But if you're open to expanding your circle, there are countless potential friends out there, many of whom are just as eager to connect as you are. Consider these tips for meeting new people and building meaningful, lasting friendships.

ARE YOU ACTUALLY PREPARED FOR ADDITIONAL COMPANIONS?

Friendship offers a lot, but it also demands certain things from you.

Are You Ready for More Friends?

Before diving into new friendships, ask yourself this question. Do you truly feel the need for more people to connect with? Consider if you can afford the time and effort required to nurture these relationships. There are factors to consider before adding new friends to your life.

Can You Invest Time?

Time is the most valuable investment in any friendship. You need to be present and actively contribute to building and maintaining the relationship. If your schedule is already packed, making time for new friends might require some adjustments.

Is Your Personality Aligned?

Your readiness for new friendships also depends on your personality. Reflect on past experiences and identify any traits that may have hindered previous relationships. Are you too assertive or too passive? Addressing these issues beforehand can prevent similar problems in new friendships.

Is Your Mindset Prepared?

Building new friendships requires emotional readiness. Are you prepared to experience joy, care, and vulnerability? Opening up to new friends means being willing to share thoughts and emotions. Ensure you're mentally prepared for this level of connection.

Are You Committed?

Friendships, while not romantic, still require commitment. You need to be there for your friends just as you expect them to be there for you. Commit to nurturing these relationships and doing what it takes to sustain them.

When it comes to fostering new friendships, it's essential to approach them with a positive and open mindset. Here are some additional aspects to consider as you navigate the realm of building and maintaining meaningful connections:

1. *Authenticity*: Be yourself and allow others to do the same. Authenticity is key to forming genuine bonds. Avoid trying to impress or conform to please others; instead, focus on being true to who you are.

2. *Shared Interests:* Look for common interests or activities that you and potential friends enjoy. Shared hobbies, passions, or even similar career paths can provide a strong foundation for friendship.

3. Communication: Effective communication is vital in any relationship. Be clear and honest in your communication, express your thoughts and feelings openly, and listen actively to what others have to say.

4. Boundaries: Respect personal boundaries and set your own boundaries as well. Understand what you're comfortable with in terms of time commitments, sharing personal information, and the level of emotional investment you're ready to make.

5. Support and Empathy: Show support and empathy towards your friends. Be there for them during challenging times, celebrate their successes, and offer a listening ear without judgment.

6. Conflict Resolution: No relationship is without occasional disagreements. Learn healthy ways to resolve conflicts, communicate your concerns calmly, and be willing to compromise when needed.

7. Quality Over Quantity: Focus on building

a few close and meaningful friendships rather than trying to have a large circle of acquaintances. Quality friendships often bring more fulfillment and support.

8. *Consistency:* Regularly nurture your friendships by staying in touch, checking in on each other, and making time for shared activities or conversations.

By approaching friendships with sincerity, respect, and a willingness to invest time and effort, you can cultivate lasting and enriching connections in your life.

CHAPTER 12

WHERE TO SEARCH FOR COMPANIONS APPROPRIATE TO YOUR DESIRES

Finding friends who share your interests can really jazz up your friendships and keep them going strong. Check out these neat ideas on where and how to meet like-minded pals.

Volunteer Groups: Get involved in volunteer

organizations to do some good while bonding with people who care about the same causes as you.

Book Clubs and Literary Events: Dive into book clubs or literary events if you're a book lover. Swap book recommendations, chat about your favorite reads, and bond over your shared love for stories.

Fitness Classes or Sports Teams: Stay active and make new buddies by joining fitness classes or sports teams. It's a fun way to stay healthy and connect with people who share your passion for staying active.

Art and Creativity Workshops: Let your creativity flow in art classes or workshops. Connect with fellow art enthusiasts and express yourself through art, music, writing, or any form of creative expression.

Networking Events: Attend professional gatherings related to your field or interests to meet colleagues and potential friends who share your passions.

Local Community Events: Keep an eye out for local festivals, fairs, and cultural events where you can mingle with diverse people and expand your social circle.

Online Communities: Dive into online forums, social media groups, or niche websites to connect with people who share your hobbies and interests. Engage in discussions and share experiences with like-minded individuals.

Travel Groups: If you're a travel enthusiast, join travel groups or clubs to meet fellow adventurers and explore new destinations together.

By actively seeking out these opportunities, you can meet awesome people who vibe with your interests and values, leading to meaningful and long-lasting friendships.

And here are some additional tips for nurturing your friendships.

Create Memories Together: Plan fun activities with your friends to create shared memories and strengthen your bond.

Open Communication: Be honest, listen attentively, and express yourself clearly to foster healthy and open friendships.

Support Each Other: Show empathy and be

there for your friends during both good times and challenges.

Respect Boundaries: Honor your friends' personal space and preferences.

Celebrate Achievements: Cheer on your friends' successes and milestones.

Resolve Conflicts Peacefully: Handle disagreements with understanding and respect.

Stay Connected: Keep in touch regularly, even if it's through technology.

Be Authentic: Be yourself and encourage authenticity in your friendships.

Forgive and Accept: Let go of grudges and embrace understanding.

Quality Over Quantity: Focus on nurturing quality friendships that bring positivity to your life.

Prioritizing these aspects will help you cultivate strong, supportive, and enduring friendships.

WHERE TO EXPAND YOUR SOCIAL NETWORK

Having a big group of friends can really boost your social standing within the community. It's not just about perception; being part of a large social circle also increases your chances of finding a potential lifelong partner.

Research suggests that over 75% of people find their partners within their own social circles. It makes sense, right? Building a romantic connection with someone you already know is often easier than trying to meet new people outside your circle.

So, maybe it's time to expand your social horizons. Here's how you can start:

Firstly, focus on strengthening your existing friendships. It's often simpler and more convenient to deepen your bonds with current friends than to start from scratch. You don't need to go overboard; just take small steps to grow closer with them.

Within your social circle, there might be friends who don't know each other yet. You can play the role of a connector, introducing them to each other and fostering new connections. Organize thoughtful surprises or fun activities like birthday parties or reunions to bring everyone closer together.

And don't forget about making new friends. While it's not always easy, reaching out to new people is an effective way to expand your social network. Be open to rejections or initial uneasiness; not everyone is quick to make new friends. Stay flexible, learn to connect with different personalities, and soon enough, you'll expand your circle with genuine connections.

Expanding your social circle can be an exciting journey filled with opportunities to connect with diverse personalities and create meaningful relationships. Here are some additional tips and insights to help you navigate and thrive in your social endeavors:

1. Embrace Diversity: One of the most enriching aspects of expanding your social circle is encountering people from different backgrounds, cultures, and perspectives. Embrace this diversity as it can broaden your horizons, challenge your assumptions, and foster personal growth. Be open to learning from others' experiences and be respectful of their unique identities.

2. Attend Social Events: Make an effort to attend social gatherings, parties, or community events where you can meet new people. These settings provide casual and relaxed environments for initiating conversations and

building connections. Don't be afraid to introduce yourself and strike up conversations based on shared interests or common experiences.

3. Explore Shared Hobbies: Engage in activities or hobbies that align with your interests and passions. Whether it's joining a cooking class, art workshop, hiking group, or dance club, participating in shared activities allows you to connect with like-minded individuals who share your enthusiasm.

4. Be Approachable and Friendly: Your demeanor plays a significant role in attracting new friends. Be approachable, friendly, and open to interactions. Smile, make eye contact, and show genuine interest in getting to know others. A warm and welcoming attitude can go a long way in building rapport and forming connections.

5. Utilize Social Media: While face-to-face interactions are valuable, social media platforms can also be powerful tools for expanding your social circle. Join online communities, forums, or groups related to your interests

or hobbies. Engage in discussions, share your thoughts and experiences, and connect with individuals who resonate with you.

6. Attend Workshops or Seminars: Professional workshops, seminars, or networking events are not only beneficial for career growth but also for expanding your social network. Connect with colleagues or attendees who share common professional interests or career goals. Building professional relationships can often lead to meaningful friendships outside of work.

7. Volunteer for Causes You Care About: Volunteering for charitable organizations or community initiatives not only allows you to contribute to a meaningful cause but also exposes you to like-minded individuals who share your values and passions. Collaborating on volunteer projects can lead to lasting friendships built on shared values and altruism.

8. Be Patient and Persistent: Building new friendships takes time and effort, so be patient with the process. Not every interaction

will result in an instant connection, and that's okay. Stay persistent in your efforts to meet new people, nurture relationships, and create a supportive social network over time.

Remember that genuine friendships are built on mutual respect, trust, and shared experiences. By taking proactive steps, staying open-minded, and being authentic in your interactions, you'll create a vibrant and fulfilling social life enriched by diverse connections and lasting friendships.

MAKING FRIENDS ON THE CYBERSPACE

Connecting with new friends in the online world is like opening a door to a whole new realm of possibilities. It's not just about expanding your social circle but also about experiencing a vibrant virtual community where friendships can blossom. Here's a casual take on how you can navigate this digital landscape and make meaningful connections:

Imagine stepping into a world where friendships transcend borders and time zones. This isn't some distant future or afterlife; it's the present, and it's buzzing with life 24/7. The Internet is your gateway to this world, offering a myriad of options to meet new friends and forge connections across continents.

In today's digital age, you've probably dipped your toes into online interactions and made friends virtually. Social networking sites like Facebook, Twitter, and others have become hubs for global connections. They're not just platforms; they're vibrant communities where you can explore shared interests, engage in discussions, and meet like-minded individuals.

One of the perks of online friendships is the diversity you encounter. You'll interact with people from various backgrounds, cultures, and perspectives, enriching your understanding of the world. These platforms not only connect you with potential friends but also offer insights into their lives through profile views and shared content.

Blogging is another avenue where friendships flourish. Your blog becomes a space to share your thoughts, ideas, and experiences. As readers resonate with your writings, they start following you, leaving comments, and engaging in meaningful conversations. It's a natural progression from readers to friends as you bond over shared interests and perspectives.

YouTube marketing is also a trend worth exploring. By creating compelling videos that resonate with viewers, you attract an audience that seeks more from you. This can lead to interactions, discussions, and ultimately, friendships built on mutual interests and admiration.

While online friendships offer immense possibilities, they come with their nuances. Building trust and understanding takes time, especially when bridging cultural and geographical gaps. It's essential to approach online interactions with caution, respect, and an open mind.

Trust is a cornerstone of any relationship,

including online friendships. Both parties navigate a landscape where intentions may be genuine yet hidden behind screens. It's a dance of communication, transparency, and mutual respect that gradually paves the way for sincere connections.

Navigating the complexities of online friendships requires patience, empathy, and a willingness to bridge differences. As you traverse this digital realm, remember that every interaction, conversation, and connection adds depth to your social landscape. It's a journey of exploration, learning, and building bridges that transcend virtual boundaries.

Navigating the world of online friendships is like embarking on a digital adventure, full of surprises, challenges, and moments of genuine connection. Let's delve deeper into this virtual realm and explore the intricacies of forging meaningful relationships online.

The internet acts as a vast playground where individuals from all walks of life converge, sharing their stories, passions, and interests. Social media platforms like Instagram,

TikTok, and Reddit have become digital gathering spots where friendships spark over shared hobbies, fandoms, and experiences.

Picture yourself scrolling through a feed filled with posts, videos, and comments that resonate with your interests. Each interaction, whether a like, a comment, or a shared meme, is a thread weaving the fabric of potential friendships. It's a dynamic space where conversations flow freely, transcending geographical barriers.

Online communities centered around niche interests offer a haven for like-minded individuals to connect. Whether you're passionate about gaming, cooking, fitness, or vintage fashion, there's a virtual tribe waiting to welcome you with open arms. These communities foster a sense of belonging and camaraderie as members bond over their common passions.

One of the joys of online friendships is the spontaneity and serendipity of encounters. You might stumble upon a post or a video that sparks a conversation, leading to a newfound friendship. The digital landscape is teeming with opportunities to meet fascinating people who broaden your horizons and enrich your life.

Blogging continues to be a powerful platform for building connections. As you share your thoughts, experiences, and creative endeavors, you invite others into your world. Engaging with readers through comments, emails, or social media channels creates a dialogue that transcends the written word, fostering genuine connections.

Podcasts have also emerged as a medium for forging connections. Hosting or participating in podcast discussions allows you to connect with listeners who resonate with your topics and perspectives. It's a collaborative space where conversations evolve into friendships grounded in shared interests and mutual respect.

Navigating the nuances of online friendships involves balancing authenticity with digital etiquette. Being genuine, respectful, and empathetic in your interactions fosters trust and rapport. It's about cultivating a digital presence that reflects your values while remaining open to diverse perspectives and experiences.

While online friendships offer vast opportunities for connection, it's essential to approach them with mindfulness and discernment. Building meaningful relationships requires time, effort, and a willingness to navigate the complexities of virtual communication.

In conclusion, the digital landscape is a playground of possibilities for fostering friendships that transcend borders and bring people together based on shared passions and interests. Embrace the adventure, cherish the connections you make, and let every interaction be a stepping stone toward meaningful relationships in the online world.

HOW TO MAKE FRIENDS IN SOCIAL EVENTS?

Parties and social gatherings are such a blast! They're perfect for catching up with old pals, hanging out with your current crew, and even making new friends. But sometimes, negative vibes can sneak in and put a damper on the fun. Here are some tips to keep the good times rolling without letting negativity spoil the party.

When conversations take a turn toward gossip or unhelpful topics, gently steer the discussion toward something more positive and interesting. It can be tricky to do this tactfully, but remember, your friends want a good time too. Find smooth ways to shift the conversation without anyone feeling left out or ignored. This way, you'll keep the vibe positive and engaging throughout the event.

If you're the host, it's your job to set the tone and keep the energy high. Think of fun conversation starters and enjoyable activities to keep everyone entertained. Plan ahead so that everything runs smoothly, and avoid diving into gossipy or controversial topics. Bringing humor into the mix can also keep the atmosphere light and enjoyable for everyone.

As a guest, you have a role too. Be mindful of the conversations you join, and aim to listen more than you talk. Show genuine interest in others by actively listening to what they have to say. Remember, everyone wants to be heard, so give your friends the gift of your attention and time.

Social events are not just about having a good time; they're also opportunities to improve your social skills and learn from different perspectives. Embrace these experiences, enjoy the company of your friends, and handle yourself with respect and consideration for others. Cheers to fun-filled gatherings and meaningful connections!

When it comes to social events, there's always more to explore and enjoy. Here are some additional tips and insights to make your gatherings even more memorable:

1. Create a Welcoming Atmosphere: As a host, go the extra mile to make your guests feel comfortable and welcome. Pay attention to details like music, lighting, and seating arrangements to set a warm and inviting ambiance.

2. Encourage Inclusive Conversations: Keep conversations inclusive by involving everyone and avoiding topics that

might alienate or make others uncomfortable. Foster a sense of belonging and camaraderie among your guests.

3.   Plan Interactive Activities: Organize interactive games or activities that encourage collaboration and laughter. This can be anything from group charades to a friendly trivia quiz. Fun activities help break the ice and create lasting memories.

4.   Offer Delicious Refreshments: Food and drinks can be a highlight of any gathering. Provide a variety of tasty refreshments, including snacks, appetizers, and beverages that cater to different preferences and dietary needs.

5.   Capture the Moment: Take photos or videos during the event to capture the fun and excitement. Share these moments with your guests afterward, creating a sense of connection and nostalgia.

6.   Express Gratitude: Show appreciation to your guests for attending by thanking them sincerely. A small gesture

like a handwritten thank-you note or a thoughtful parting gift can leave a lasting impression.

7.   Follow Up Afterward: After the event, follow up with your friends to express how much you enjoyed their company. It's a great way to strengthen bonds and keep the positive energy flowing beyond the gathering.

Remember, the essence of a successful social event lies in creating a space where everyone feels valued, engaged, and uplifted. Enjoy the process of connecting with others, and cherish the moments of joy and laughter shared with friends old and new.

TIPS FOR STRENGTHENING FRIENDSHIP BONDS

Building strong friendships is an ongoing process that goes beyond just meeting someone new. It's about nurturing and growing those connections into deeper, more meaningful relationships.

Continuing friendships requires finding common ground that strengthens your bond.

When you discover shared interests like music, art, dancing, or travel, use these as opportunities to deepen your friendship. For example, if you both love the same band, attending concerts together can be a fun way to enjoy your shared passion while strengthening your friendship.

In today's digital age, staying connected with your friends has become easier than ever. You can call, message, or chat with them regularly to keep the communication alive and thriving. Utilize technology to your advantage, whether it's through video calls or emails, to maintain a strong connection despite busy schedules.

Inviting your new friends to social gatherings is another great way to solidify your bond. It not only allows them to see how you interact with others but also helps them integrate into your social circle and build friendships with other people you know. This inclusivity fosters trust and confidence in your friendship.

Overall, the key is to actively engage with your friends, stay in touch through various communication channels, and include them in your social activities to nurture and grow your friendships over time.

Creating lasting friendships goes beyond just initial meetings; it involves ongoing effort and genuine connection. One way to deepen these bonds is through shared experiences. Consider planning outings or activities that align with your common interests. Whether it's exploring new hiking trails, attending art workshops together, or trying out new restaurants, these shared moments can strengthen your friendship.

Another aspect to consider is being there for your friends during both good times and challenging moments. Showing empathy, offering support, and being a reliable presence can greatly enhance the trust and closeness in your relationships. Remember to listen actively, express your care and concern, and be willing to lend a helping hand when needed.

Communication is also vital in maintaining strong friendships. Be open, honest, and transparent in your conversations. Share your thoughts, feelings, and experiences with your friends, and encourage them to do the same. Effective communication helps in resolving misunderstandings, addressing concerns, and deepening understanding between friends.

Building trust is a fundamental part of any friendship. Consistency, reliability, and honesty contribute to building a strong foundation of trust. Keep your promises, respect your friends' privacy and boundaries, and be dependable in your actions. Trust is earned over time through consistent and positive interactions.

Celebrating each other's successes and milestones is another way to foster positivity and closeness in friendships. Whether it's congratulating a friend on a promotion, celebrating a birthday, or cheering them on during achievements, showing genuine happiness and support strengthens the bond between friends.

Lastly, remember that friendships evolve and change over time. People grow, interests may shift, and life circumstances can vary. Embrace these changes with flexibility and understanding, and continue to invest in your friendships by staying connected, being present, and nurturing the bonds that matter to you.

FINAL STRENGTH

The world's population is booming, which might not be everyone's cup of tea, but it's actually something to be happy about. With so many people around, you've got plenty of chances to meet folks who could become great friends.

Friends are such a big part of our lives, right? They're there for us through thick and thin, offering support, comfort, even a bit of tough love when needed. They're the ones we laugh with, cry with, and share life's ups and downs.

Building lasting friendships is a journey. It's about being friendly, both in how you act and how you feel. Smiling, chatting, being patient with quirks, accepting people for who they are — these are all ways to not only make friends but to keep them close.

Choosing your friends wisely matters too. Surrounding yourself with positive influences can shape who you are. It's like they say, "Show me your friends, and I'll show you your future."

Stay genuine and consistent in your friendships. Don't be the friend who's all in at first and then disappears when things get real. Show love and understanding, celebrate strengths, and support each other through challenges.

Treat your friends with respect and kindness. They're not there to serve you but to share life's journey with you. Don't take them for granted; appreciate and value them.

Don't limit yourself when it comes to

friends. They're everywhere, waiting to be discovered. Break down walls, build bridges, and embrace the joy of connecting with others. Life's too short not to cherish the people who make it brighter.

I hope this little guide helps you navigate the world of friendships with confidence and warmth. Here's to finding and keeping those special people in your life — your friends! All the best to you!

Friendships are like flowers that bloom with care and attention. Just like you nurture a plant with water and sunlight, you nurture your friendships with love, understanding, and shared experiences. It's not just about having a large circle of acquaintances; it's about cultivating meaningful connections that enrich your life.

One of the key ingredients in a lasting friendship is trust. Trust forms the foundation on which you build your bond. When you trust your friends and they trust you, it creates a sense of security and authenticity in your relationship. You can be yourself, share your thoughts and feelings openly, and know that your friend will be there for you no matter what.

Communication is another vital aspect of friendship. It's not just about talking; it's about truly listening and understanding each other. Take the time to listen to your friends' stories, concerns, and dreams. Show empathy, offer support, and be a reliable confidant. Likewise, express yourself honestly and openly. Communication strengthens your connection and builds mutual respect.

Friendships also thrive on shared experiences. Whether it's going on adventures together, trying new activities, or simply spending quality time chatting over coffee, these shared moments create lasting memories. They strengthen your bond and give you a treasure trove of stories to reminisce about in the future.

It's important to be there for your friends during both the good times and the challenging times. Celebrate their successes, be a shoulder to lean on during tough moments, and cheer them on in their endeavors. Your support and encouragement mean the world to them.

As you navigate friendships, remember that it's okay to have different types of friends for different aspects of your life. You might have friends you share hobbies with, work friends, childhood friends, and so on. Each friend brings something unique to your life, enriching it in diverse ways.

Lastly, cherish your friendships and express gratitude for the wonderful people in your life. Let them know how much they mean to you and make an effort to show your appreciation regularly. A heartfelt gesture or a simple "thank you" can go a long way in strengthening your friendships.

So, here's to cultivating beautiful friendships that bring joy, laughter, and support into your life!

SECTION 3 - FROM FRIENDS TO LOVERS

CAN IT BE DONE?

Navigating the "friend zone" can feel like a maze, right? You're into someone, hoping for more, but they see you as just a buddy. It's frustrating, isn't it? But don't worry, we'll tackle this together!

Many folks, both guys, and gals, have been in your shoes. Trying everything to shift from friend to more-than-friend status, yet nothing seems to click. And the fear of ruining the friendship? It's real! No one wants that.

Imagine being so close to someone, sharing your world, yet what you crave is beyond reach. If you're reading this, chances are:

a. You fancy a friend and want to take things up a notch.

b. You used to be romantic with someone who now prefers the "just friends" label.

c. You've been here before and want to avoid the friend zone in future relationships.

d. You've seen others go through this, and you're determined to stay out of that zone.

This guide will equip you with savvy insights and clever seduction tricks to escape the friend zone or avoid it altogether. Ever wondered why this "friend zone" situation happens so often? We'll unravel that mystery too!

Starting with quick and easy tips you can try right away, we'll move on to more advanced strategies. It might take a bit more effort, but trust me, the results will blow your mind!

Before diving into tactics, there's a crucial discussion we need to have. Don't skip any part of this guide—it's all key to maximizing your chances of success in navigating the friend zone.

IS IT WORTH THE INVESTMENT?

Is this whole thing worth it, really? Before diving into the strategies laid out here, let's ask some important questions.

First off, what do you actually want from this, and why? It's crucial to be clear about your desires and motivations. Do you envision a full-blown relationship with your friend, or maybe a long-term "friends with benefits" setup? Or are you just after a fleeting fling, a night of passion perhaps? Is curiosity driving you—just to see what it'd be like to take things to another level?

Consider the value of your current friendship. Is it worth risking for a short-lived romance, especially a fleeting sexual encounter? Reflect on your intentions. Are they driven by jealousy, insecurity, ego, or external pressures?

Be honest with yourself. Don't sugarcoat it; that'll only backfire later on. From my experience, I'd advise against fleeting affairs. If you cherish your friendship, proceed only if you genuinely seek a long-term connection.

Now, about wasting time—let's dig deeper. Assess if your friend aligns with your desires. Look at her past relationships, her personality, her treatment of others. Is she open to the type of relationship you seek? Don't force a square peg into a round hole; it rarely ends well.

Evaluate her values, her non-negotiables in a partner. Does she prioritize cultural, religious, or lifestyle compatibility? Are you both on the same page? Trying to fit where you don't belong isn't just futile—it's draining.

Remember, life's too rich to fixate on one person. Be real about compatibility, for both your sakes. If after all this, pursuing more than friendship still seems wise, then let's dive in!

When it comes to navigating relationships, especially those with friends that you'd like to take to the next level, there's often a blend of excitement and uncertainty. It's like stepping into uncharted territory while holding onto a familiar hand. That mix of anticipation and caution is what makes these moments so intriguing yet challenging.

Let's delve into another aspect—communication. How do you express your feelings without risking the friendship? It's like walking on a tightrope; one wrong step, and the balance could tip. This is where understanding comes into play—knowing when and how to communicate your desires respectfully and honestly. It's about creating a safe space for both parties to express their thoughts and feelings without fear of judgment or rejection.

And what about timing? Timing can be everything, yet it's also unpredictable. Sometimes, the stars align, and the moment feels right. Other times, it's a delicate dance of waiting for the right opportunity without rushing or pushing too hard.

Let's not forget about emotions—the roller-coaster ride of excitement, nervousness, hope, and doubt. It's like being on an emotional seesaw, trying to find that perfect balance between expressing your feelings and respecting the other person's boundaries and comfort level.

In the end, navigating the transition from friends to something more requires a delicate balance of communication, timing, understanding, and emotional intelligence. It's about being true to yourself while also being considerate of the other person's feelings and perspective. And above all, it's about approaching the situation with sincerity, respect, and a genuine desire for mutual happiness and fulfillment.

CHOOSING THE RIGHT PLAN OF ATTACK

Alright, before diving into the strategies laid out here, let's take a moment to understand where you're at with your friend. What's the vibe like between you two? How does she see you, and how does she define your relationship?

Usually, these situations fall into one of three categories...

1. She sees you strictly as a buddy, with no romantic vibes involved.
2. You're a great friend to her, and maybe there's a hint of attraction there, past or present.
3. She might even see you like a brother or one of her gal pals.

Understanding which of these dynamics fits your situation helps in plotting your "friends to more" strategy. If you're not totally sure yet, don't sweat it. As we go through this report, things will start to clear up.

Next, let's peek at your actions and interactions with her so far. What signals have you sent her?

1. You've always kept it strictly friendly, never hinting at anything more.
2. You've playfully or seriously flirted, testing the waters.

3. You've been upfront, either verbally or through actions, about your feelings or desire for more.

Knowing where you stand and how you've approached things helps tailor your approach. Since I can't chat with you in person, I'll share techniques that fit all these scenarios. You can then pick what suits your situation best as you go through the report.

When considering how to proceed with turning a friendship into something more, it's crucial to also think about her perspective and feelings. How does she perceive your interactions? Is she open to the idea of taking your relationship to the next level, or does she seem content with things as they are?

Here are a few key points to ponder:

1. Her Signals: Has she given you any signals that she might be interested in more than friendship? Maybe she's dropped hints or flirted back when you've tested the waters. On the flip side, has she

ever mentioned wanting to keep things strictly platonic?

2.   Emotional Connection: Consider the emotional connection between you two. Do you share deep conversations and confide in each other? Is there a sense of trust and comfort that goes beyond typical friendships?

3.   Physical Boundaries: Pay attention to physical boundaries. Have there been moments of physical closeness or intimacy that hint at a potential for romance? Or has she maintained clear boundaries, indicating a desire to keep things non-romantic?

4.   Past Experiences: Reflect on any past experiences you've had together. Have there been moments of tension or chemistry that could suggest underlying romantic feelings? Or has your friendship always felt purely platonic?

By taking these factors into account, you can gain a better understanding of where you both stand and how to approach the situation sensitively and respectfully. Remember, communication and mutual understanding are key foundations for navigating the transition from friends to something more.

BENEFITS OF BEING "FRIENDS FIRST"

It's ideal to avoid finding yourself in the "friend zone" with someone you're attracted to, unless you've consciously decided that pursuing a deeper connection isn't what you want with that person. There are strategies you can employ right from the start to steer clear of the "friend zone" when interacting with women.

I'll delve into these strategies later on in this report.

However, as frustrating as it can be to remain "just friends" with someone you desire more from, there are actually some perks to being in the "friend zone." If you're already in this situation, you can leverage these benefits to your advantage.

Firstly, being close friends with a woman often means she already trusts you. Trust is a crucial aspect of relationships, particularly for women. In this regard, you're ahead of many other guys she may have dated or will date in the future.

Additionally, being friends decreases the likelihood of facing rejection compared to strangers who approach her for a date. Lastly, being good friends grants you a deeper understanding of her personality, preferences, and what she seeks in a partner. This insight gives you an edge that other guys don't have before they start dating her.

All these advantages give you a unique position. I'll guide you on how to utilize these benefits effectively as you navigate through the relevant sections of this report.

When it comes to navigating the dynamics of friendship and attraction, it's important to strike a balance between expressing your interest and respecting the existing friendship. Here are some additional insights to consider:

1. Open Communication: Honest and open communication is key. If you're interested in more than friendship with someone, it's okay to express that respectfully. However, it's also crucial to be understanding if the feelings aren't reciprocated. Clear communication can prevent misunderstandings and maintain the friendship even if romantic feelings aren't mutual.

2. Respect Boundaries: Everyone has boundaries, and it's essential to respect them. If your friend has indicated that they prefer to remain friends, it's important not to push for more or make them uncomfortable. Respecting their bound-

aries shows maturity and strengthens trust in the friendship.

3. Focus on Mutual Enjoyment: Enjoying each other's company and shared interests is a cornerstone of friendship. Emphasize activities and conversations that both of you find enjoyable and fulfilling. Building on these shared experiences can deepen the bond between you without necessarily crossing into romantic territory.

4. Emotional Support: Friendship often involves providing emotional support and being there for each other during tough times. Show empathy, listen actively, and offer assistance when needed. Being a reliable and supportive friend can strengthen your connection and create a foundation of trust and understanding.

5. Self-Reflection: Take time to reflect on your own feelings and motivations. Understand why you value the friendship and what you're looking for in a relationship. This self-awareness can

guide your actions and decisions, ensuring that you prioritize the well-being of both yourself and your friend.

By approaching the situation with sensitivity, clear communication, and respect for boundaries, you can navigate the "friend zone" with grace and maintain a meaningful connection with your friend, whether it evolves into something more or remains a cherished friendship.

GETTING INTO THE "FRIEND ZONE"

Sure thing, here's the rewrite:

You know, when it comes to stepping out of that "friend zone," it's key to figure out how you ended up there in the first place. And let's be real, a lot of guys find themselves in that spot because, well, they put themselves there. But hey, it's not all on them.

Sadly, society kind of nudges guys into this

idea that being friends first is the way to go. But let me tell you, that's often far from the truth.

Guys often think that if they play the friendship card, spending all this time together will magically make her see them in a different light. Newsflash: it hardly ever works. What really matters isn't the quantity of time spent but the quality of those moments.

And here's the kicker—women often say they want to start as friends, but that's not the whole story. It's like a script we all follow to feel better about things, you know? But deep down, many women appreciate a guy who's upfront and takes the lead.

Now, what if a guy didn't intentionally choose the "friends first" route? How does he still land in that zone? It's usually because of subtle things that keep reinforcing the friend vibe.

Take flirting, for example. If you're not flirting at all or keeping things too safe, you might as well be shouting, "Just friends!" from the rooftops. And let's face it, being too comfortable can seal the deal. If you're Netflix-and-chilling like buddies, chances are she sees you more as a comfy couch than a potential flame.

Plus, women thrive on emotional highs. If you're not giving her those roller-coaster moments, she might think, "Eh, why change a good thing?" And bam, you're officially the mayor of Friend Zone City.

So, it's about finding that balance between being genuine and adding a spark. I'll dive deeper into these tactics next.

Now, let's talk about one of the most common pitfalls that land guys in the friend zone: not being assertive enough. Picture this —you're hanging out with her, maybe watching a movie or grabbing coffee, and you're doing everything to play it cool. But here's the thing: being too chill can send the wrong message. It's like you're saying, "I'm cool just being buddies forever."

On the flip side, being assertive doesn't mean being pushy or disrespectful. It's about showing her that you're interested in more than just friendship without making it awkward.

Maybe it's a gentle touch on the arm during a conversation or a sincere compliment that goes beyond the usual friendly banter.

Another common misstep is not setting boundaries. It's great to be there for her, listen to her problems, and offer support. But if it's always a one-way street where you're the go-to emotional support without any romantic potential, you're solidifying your status as the BFF.

So, how do you break out of this pattern? It starts with communication. Yes, I know, it sounds cliché, but hear me out. It's about being honest about your feelings and intentions without making it a grand confession. It could be as simple as saying, "You know, I've really enjoyed our time together, and I'd like to explore something more than just friendship if you're open to it."

Now, I get it. That can be nerve-wracking. But remember, vulnerability can be attractive. It shows that you're genuine and brave enough to express yourself. And hey, if she's not on the same page, that's okay too. It's about being true to yourself and respecting her feelings.

On the flip side, if she does respond positively or shows interest, it's time to take the lead. Plan a date that's more than just the usual hangout. Show her a side of you that goes beyond the friend persona. And most importantly, keep the momentum going. Consistency in your actions and intentions can go a long way in shifting the dynamic from friends to something more.

Ultimately, breaking out of the friend zone isn't about playing games or trying to manipulate feelings. It's about authenticity, clear communication, and taking calculated risks. So, embrace the journey, learn from each interaction, and remember that sometimes, the best relationships start as unexpected twists in the friendship tale.

CHAPTER 23

GETTING OUT OF THE "FRIEND ZONE"

So, you know how sometimes, despite a guy's best efforts, he ends up in the friend zone? It's like this weird vortex where getting out seems nearly impossible. Well, unless you've got this report handy, wink wink ;-)

But seriously, let's talk about breaking free from the friend zone and staying out for good. There are a few ways to do it, and I'll share them with you. Which one you choose depends on your unique situation with her and what you both vibe with.

Here's the deal—whether we want to admit it or not, we're mostly the architects of our own friend-zoning. And guess what? We're also the ones with the keys to get out of it. Women usually won't make the first move to shift things because, let's face it, they've got plenty of guys lining up. But a good friend? That's a different story. So, it's all on us to make the change.

That's why I put together this report—to guide you through this tricky terrain so you don't feel like you're doing it solo. No more guessing games or failed attempts; let's get you out of that dreaded friend zone once and for all.

First up, let's talk about ditching the "bro" or "girl" friend vibes. It's time to shake things up—no more cozy pajama hangs or marathon movie nights. We're steering clear of those conversations that feel more like gossip sessions and activities that scream "just friends."

It's about setting a different tone, one that hints at more than friendship.

And here's a secret weapon—letting her miss you. Yep, taking a step back can work wonders. Give her some space to realize your value and maybe even stir up a little curiosity.

While you're at it, why not amp up your own life? Dive into new hobbies, meet new people, and level up your overall vibe. It's not just about looking good (though that helps); it's about showing her that you've got a life beyond being her go-to buddy.

And hey, let's not forget the power of dressing the part. Looking sharp isn't just about appearances; it's about signaling a shift in how she sees you. Plus, who doesn't love a well-groomed guy?

Now, here's a fun twist—planting the idea of "more than friends" in her mind. It's all about subtle hints and shared experiences that nudge her thoughts in a different direction without feeling forced.

And when you do spend time together, switch things up. Say goodbye to friend-zone activities and hello to "date stuff." It's about creating a new dynamic and letting her see you in a different light.

Lastly, remember that improving yourself isn't about changing who you are—it's about becoming the best version of yourself. So, let's dive in and make this journey from friends to something more an exciting adventure, shall we?

Let's delve deeper into each aspect of breaking free from the friend zone and transforming your dynamic with her:

First off, shedding the "bro" or "girl" friend label involves a subtle yet significant shift in how you interact. It's about creating a new atmosphere—one that hints at romantic potential without being overt. This means no more cozy pajama hangs or endless movie marathons. Instead, opt for outings or activities that have a more date-like vibe. Think dinner at a nice restaurant, exploring a new place together, or even just dressing up a bit more when you meet.

Creating space for her to miss you is key.

It's not about disappearing completely, but rather about striking a balance between being present and giving her room to appreciate your absence. Use this time to focus on your own interests and passions, showing her that you're a multifaceted person with a life outside of your friendship.

Leveling up your life isn't just about adding new activities—it's also about cultivating a mindset of growth and self-improvement. Take up that language class you've always wanted to try, hit the gym regularly, or delve into a hobby that challenges you. Not only will this make you more attractive in her eyes, but it'll also boost your confidence and overall well-being.

When it comes to dressing the part, think of it as a form of self-expression. Dressing well isn't just about looking good (although that certainly doesn't hurt); it's about showcasing your personality and style. Find clothing that makes you feel confident and reflects the image you want to project. Plus, a well-groomed appearance signals that you value yourself and take pride in your presentation.

Planting the idea of "more than friends" involves subtle cues and shared experiences that gently nudge her thoughts in a different direction. It's about creating moments that spark a sense of romantic possibility without coming on too strong. This could be through playful teasing, meaningful conversations, or shared adventures that deepen your connection.

And when you do spend time together, focus on creating memorable experiences. Ditch the usual friend-zone activities and opt for outings that have a romantic undertone. Whether it's a candlelit dinner, a weekend getaway, or simply enjoying each other's company in a more intimate setting, these moments help redefine your relationship dynamics.

Ultimately, the journey from friends to something more is about authenticity, communication, and mutual respect. By being true to yourself, expressing your feelings openly (but without pressure), and respecting her boundaries, you set the stage for a potential shift in your relationship. It's a process that requires patience, understanding, and a willingness to embrace change, but the rewards can be truly transformative.

PULLING OUT THE BIG GUNS: ADVANCED SEDUCTION AND PERSUASION

So, we've chatted about "planting the seed" in a woman's mind and how to get her feeling attracted to you. Shared experiences are key too, right? They make those emotional highs stick to you like glue!

Now, let's dive into how you can do all of that just by chatting with her, making it sound totally normal. You can weave this style of conversation into your hangouts or dates; it'll fit right in and amp up that romantic vibe.

We're going to use what's called "process language" or "hypnotic language," a trick from NLP and the pick-up scene. It's all about using descriptive, sensory-rich words and clever questions to stir up strong emotions in her. Then, we'll link those emotions to you, like magic.

Think of it as painting a vivid picture in her mind. Ever watched a scary movie and felt jumpy afterward, even knowing it's all pretend? That's how powerful imagination can be.

Now, think about a moment from your past that made you super happy or super sad. Remember how those feelings rush back? It's like time traveling through emotions!

And here's the kicker: when she feels something intense around you, her mind starts connecting those emotions to you. That's why shared experiences hit different, right?

So, to sum it up, if you want her to feel attraction, just guide her to relive a past moment of attraction. Easy peasy!

Imagine asking her something like, "Remember that time you were totally crushing on someone?" It's like opening a treasure chest of emotions! And as she dives into those memories, pay attention—her feelings will guide the conversation.

The key is making her feel those emotions again, vividly. If she's not quite there, gently nudge her to relive it more intensely. And remember, keep it light and fun. If she gets uncomfortable, switch gears and revisit it later.

You can use this approach to amp up feelings of romance, arousal, and yes, even love. Share your own stories or spin tales about others—it's all fair game!

Practice makes perfect, so try it out with friends or even over the phone. Before you know it, you'll be leading her on a journey of emotions that could end with that magical first kiss.

When you're ready to initiate that first kiss, remember that timing and setting play crucial roles. You want the atmosphere to be just right, with a bit of intimacy and closeness. It could be after a shared laugh, a heartfelt conversation, or a moment of quiet connection. Pay attention to her body language and cues, as they can guide you towards the perfect moment.

Start by subtly moving closer, maybe touching her arm or adjusting her hair gently. Gauge her response—if she leans in or mirrors your movements, it's a good sign that she's open to the idea. Keep the conversation light and playful, maintaining eye contact to build anticipation.

When you feel the timing is right, you can introduce the idea of the first kiss indirectly. You might say something like, "You know, talking about past first kisses always brings back those butterflies. Do you remember how your first kiss felt?" This not only keeps the conversation flowing but also sets the stage for a nostalgic and romantic mood.

As she recalls her past experiences, listen attentively and empathize with her feelings. You can share your own first kiss story, creating a sense of bonding and shared vulnerability. This gradual progression from reminiscing to personal sharing can heighten the emotional connection between you.

When the moment feels electric and charged with anticipation, go for it! Lean in slowly, giving her the opportunity to meet you halfway. A gentle and passionate first kiss can speak volumes, expressing feelings that words often struggle to convey.

Remember, every person and situation is unique, so trust your instincts and respect her boundaries. Building emotional connections takes time and patience, so enjoy the journey of discovering each other's desires and feelings.

IMPORTANCE OF THE FIRST KISS

After that first kiss, maintaining the right balance is key. You want to convey your interest and attraction without overwhelming her. This means being attentive to her signals and responses. If she indicates a need to slow down or discuss the direction of your relationship, respect her wishes and take the time to have open and honest conversations.

Communication becomes even more crucial at this stage. You can gently inquire about her feelings and thoughts regarding the kiss and where she sees things going between you. Creating a safe space for her to express herself without pressure or judgment fosters trust and emotional intimacy.

As you continue spending time together, keep the romance alive through small gestures and thoughtful actions. Surprise her with her favorite treat, send sweet messages, or plan enjoyable outings that cater to her interests. These gestures show that you value her and are invested in nurturing the connection.

Building on shared experiences remains a powerful tool. Create memorable moments together, whether it's exploring new places, trying new activities, or simply enjoying quiet moments of connection. These shared memories deepen the bond and strengthen the emotional connection between you.

It's important to maintain authenticity throughout this process. Be genuine in your words and actions, expressing your feelings sincerely. Avoid playing games or manipulating situations, as honesty and sincerity lay the foundation for a healthy and lasting relationship.

Remember, every relationship unfolds at its own pace. Respect her boundaries and desires, and let the connection evolve naturally. Building a strong emotional connection takes time, patience, and a genuine interest in understanding and appreciating each other.

When it comes to building emotional connections, it's crucial to prioritize empathy and understanding. Take the time to listen actively to her thoughts, feelings, and experiences. Show genuine interest in what she has to say, and validate her emotions by acknowledging and empathizing with them.

As you deepen your emotional connection, continue to cultivate trust and openness. Share your own thoughts, dreams, and vulnerabilities with her, creating a space for mutual honesty and intimacy. Being transparent and authentic in your communication strengthens the bond and fosters a sense of closeness.

Another important aspect is showing appreciation and gratitude. Express gratitude for the positive impact she has on your life, whether it's through her support, companionship, or shared moments of joy. Small gestures of appreciation, such as heartfelt compliments or thoughtful gestures, can go a long way in strengthening emotional connections.

Building emotional connections also involves being attuned to her needs and preferences. Pay attention to what makes her happy, what makes her feel loved and valued, and strive to incorporate those elements into your interactions. This shows that you're invested in her well-being and happiness.

It's important to navigate challenges and conflicts with empathy and maturity. Disagreements are natural in any relationship, but how you handle them can either strengthen or strain the emotional connection. Approach conflicts with a focus on understanding each other's perspectives, finding common ground, and working together towards resolution.

Creating shared goals and aspirations can

also deepen emotional connections. Collaborate on future plans, dreams, and ambitions, whether it's traveling together, pursuing common interests, or supporting each other's personal growth. Shared goals foster a sense of partnership and mutual investment in the relationship's future.

Lastly, remember that building emotional connections is an ongoing process that requires effort, patience, and dedication. It's about nurturing the bond, building trust, and fostering a deep sense of emotional intimacy over time. Stay committed to cultivating a strong emotional connection, and it will continue to flourish and strengthen your relationship.

"STICK" STRATEGIES

Here are some additional strategies to consider as you navigate the transition from friends to lovers and work towards building a lasting relationship:

1. Communication is Key: Keep the lines of communication open and honest. Talk about your feelings, desires, and expectations for the relationship. Encourage her to share her thoughts and feelings as well. Effective

communication fosters understanding and strengthens emotional bonds.

2. Respect Boundaries: Respect her boundaries and preferences. Pay attention to verbal and non-verbal cues to ensure that both of you feel comfortable and respected at all times. Consent and mutual respect are crucial elements of a healthy relationship.

3. Show Appreciation: Continuously show appreciation for her presence in your life. Express gratitude for the moments you share, the support she provides, and the happiness she brings. Small gestures of appreciation, such as thoughtful gifts or heartfelt messages, can make a significant impact.

4. Prioritize Quality Time: Make time for meaningful and enjoyable experiences together. Plan dates, outings, and activities that you both enjoy. Quality time strengthens your connection and creates cherished memories.

5. Handle Conflicts Maturely: Disagreements and conflicts are inevitable in any relationship. Approach conflicts with maturity, empathy, and a willingness to listen and understand

each other's perspectives. Find constructive ways to resolve issues and grow stronger as a couple.

6. Support Each Other's Goals: Encourage and support each other's personal and professional goals and aspirations. Be each other's cheerleader and motivator, celebrating successes and providing encouragement during challenges.

7. Maintain Independence: While building a strong emotional connection is important, it's also essential to maintain individual identities and interests. Allow each other space for personal growth, hobbies, and friendships outside the relationship.

8. Express Affection: Show affection regularly through words, gestures, and physical touch. Express your love, admiration, and affection openly and sincerely. Acts of affection reaffirm your emotional connection and deepen intimacy.

9. Continuously Work on the Relationship: Relationships require ongoing effort and commitment. Continuously work on strengthening

your bond, addressing challenges, and nurturing a loving and fulfilling connection.

By implementing these strategies and staying committed to nurturing your relationship, you can increase the likelihood of building a strong, lasting emotional connection with your friend turned lover.